50 Heart Healthy Recipes for Home

By: Kelly Johnson

Table of Contents

- Baked Salmon with Lemon and Dill
- Quinoa and Black Bean Stuffed Bell Peppers
- Grilled Chicken Breast with Herb Salad
- Mediterranean Chickpea Salad
- Spinach and Feta Turkey Burgers
- Roasted Vegetable and Lentil Salad
- Lemon Garlic Shrimp with Zucchini Noodles
- Baked Cod with Tomatoes and Olives
- Turkey and Vegetable Stir-Fry
- Caprese Stuffed Avocados
- Kale and White Bean Soup
- Grilled Vegetable Skewers
- Herb-Roasted Chicken Thighs
- Cauliflower Rice Stir-Fry
- Tuna and White Bean Salad
- Stuffed Portobello Mushrooms with Spinach and Feta
- Greek Chicken Souvlaki with Tzatziki Sauce
- Lentil and Vegetable Curry
- Lemon Herb Grilled Tilapia
- Turkey and Quinoa Meatballs
- Greek Salad with Grilled Chicken
- Ratatouille with Herbed Quinoa
- Baked Sweet Potatoes with Black Bean Salsa
- Spicy Garlic Shrimp with Brown Rice
- Mediterranean Veggie Wrap with Hummus
- Grilled Lemon Herb Chicken Skewers
- Black Bean and Corn Salad with Cilantro Lime Dressing
- Turkey Chili with Kidney Beans
- Balsamic Glazed Salmon with Asparagus
- Roasted Brussels Sprouts with Garlic and Parmesan
- Lemon Herb Baked Cod
- Quinoa and Vegetable Stuffed Peppers
- Grilled Vegetable Quinoa Salad
- Herb-Marinated Grilled Chicken Breast
- Spicy Black Bean and Vegetable Soup

- Greek Yogurt Chicken Salad Wraps
- Lemon Garlic Shrimp and Broccoli Stir-Fry
- Turkey and Spinach Stuffed Mushrooms
- Mediterranean Tuna Salad Lettuce Wraps
- Herb-Roasted Turkey Breast
- Roasted Cauliflower and Chickpea Salad
- Grilled Lemon Herb Salmon
- Lentil and Vegetable Stuffed Bell Peppers
- Baked Chicken with Tomato and Basil
- Quinoa and Kale Salad with Lemon Vinaigrette
- Grilled Vegetable Quinoa Bowls
- Turkey and Vegetable Skillet
- Lemon Herb Baked Chicken Thighs
- Mediterranean Eggplant and Tomato Bake
- Herb-Marinated Grilled Pork Tenderloin

Baked Salmon with Lemon and Dill

Ingredients:

- 4 salmon fillets (about 6 ounces each)
- Salt and pepper to taste
- 2 tablespoons olive oil
- 2 tablespoons freshly squeezed lemon juice
- Zest of 1 lemon
- 2 cloves garlic, minced
- 2 tablespoons fresh dill, chopped
- Lemon slices for garnish
- Fresh dill sprigs for garnish

Instructions:

1. Preheat your oven to 375°F (190°C). Line a baking dish with parchment paper or lightly grease it with olive oil.
2. Pat the salmon fillets dry with paper towels and season both sides with salt and pepper.
3. In a small bowl, whisk together the olive oil, lemon juice, lemon zest, minced garlic, and chopped dill.
4. Place the salmon fillets in the prepared baking dish and pour the lemon-dill mixture evenly over the top of each fillet, using a spoon to spread it if necessary.
5. Place a few lemon slices on top of each fillet for added flavor and presentation.
6. Bake the salmon in the preheated oven for 12-15 minutes, or until the salmon is cooked through and flakes easily with a fork. Cooking time may vary depending on the thickness of your salmon fillets.
7. Once the salmon is done, remove it from the oven and garnish with fresh dill sprigs.
8. Serve the baked salmon hot with your favorite sides, such as roasted vegetables, rice, or a salad.

Enjoy your delicious baked salmon with lemon and dill!

Quinoa and Black Bean Stuffed Bell Peppers

Ingredients:

- 4 large bell peppers (any color), halved and seeds removed
- 1 cup quinoa, rinsed
- 2 cups vegetable broth or water
- 1 can (15 ounces) black beans, drained and rinsed
- 1 cup corn kernels (fresh, frozen, or canned)
- 1 small onion, finely chopped
- 2 cloves garlic, minced
- 1 teaspoon ground cumin
- 1 teaspoon chili powder
- 1/2 teaspoon smoked paprika (optional)
- Salt and pepper to taste
- 1 cup shredded cheese (cheddar, mozzarella, or your choice)
- Fresh cilantro or parsley for garnish (optional)
- Avocado slices for serving (optional)
- Salsa or sour cream for serving (optional)

Instructions:

1. Preheat your oven to 375°F (190°C).
2. In a medium saucepan, bring the vegetable broth or water to a boil. Add the quinoa, reduce the heat to low, cover, and simmer for about 15 minutes, or until the quinoa is cooked and the liquid is absorbed. Remove from heat and let it sit covered for 5 minutes, then fluff with a fork.
3. While the quinoa is cooking, heat a tablespoon of olive oil in a large skillet over medium heat. Add the chopped onion and cook until it becomes translucent, about 3-4 minutes. Add the minced garlic and cook for another 1-2 minutes.
4. Add the cooked quinoa, black beans, corn kernels, ground cumin, chili powder, smoked paprika (if using), salt, and pepper to the skillet. Stir well to combine and cook for an additional 2-3 minutes to allow the flavors to meld.
5. Arrange the halved bell peppers in a baking dish, cut side up. Spoon the quinoa and black bean mixture evenly into each pepper half, pressing down gently to pack it in.
6. Cover the baking dish with aluminum foil and bake in the preheated oven for 25-30 minutes, or until the bell peppers are tender.

7. Remove the foil from the baking dish, sprinkle the stuffed bell peppers with shredded cheese, and return them to the oven. Bake for an additional 5-10 minutes, or until the cheese is melted and bubbly.
8. Once done, remove the stuffed bell peppers from the oven and let them cool slightly before serving.
9. Garnish with fresh cilantro or parsley, avocado slices, and serve with salsa or sour cream on the side, if desired.

Enjoy your delicious quinoa and black bean stuffed bell peppers!

Grilled Chicken Breast with Herb Salad

Ingredients:

For the grilled chicken:

- 4 boneless, skinless chicken breasts
- 2 tablespoons olive oil
- 2 cloves garlic, minced
- 1 teaspoon dried oregano
- 1 teaspoon dried thyme
- Salt and pepper to taste

For the herb salad:

- 4 cups mixed fresh herbs (such as parsley, cilantro, mint, and basil), roughly chopped
- 1 cup cherry tomatoes, halved
- 1/2 red onion, thinly sliced
- 1 cucumber, diced
- Juice of 1 lemon
- 2 tablespoons extra virgin olive oil
- Salt and pepper to taste

Instructions:

1. Preheat your grill to medium-high heat.
2. In a small bowl, whisk together the olive oil, minced garlic, dried oregano, dried thyme, salt, and pepper to create a marinade for the chicken.
3. Place the chicken breasts in a shallow dish or a resealable plastic bag. Pour the marinade over the chicken, making sure each breast is evenly coated. Allow the chicken to marinate for at least 30 minutes, or refrigerate for up to 4 hours for maximum flavor.
4. While the chicken is marinating, prepare the herb salad. In a large mixing bowl, combine the mixed fresh herbs, cherry tomatoes, red onion, and diced cucumber.
5. In a small bowl, whisk together the lemon juice, extra virgin olive oil, salt, and pepper to create a simple dressing for the salad.

6. Pour the dressing over the herb salad and toss gently to coat all the ingredients. Set the salad aside while you grill the chicken.
7. Once the grill is hot, remove the chicken breasts from the marinade and shake off any excess. Place the chicken breasts on the grill and cook for 6-8 minutes per side, or until the chicken is cooked through and no longer pink in the center. The internal temperature should reach 165°F (75°C).
8. Once the chicken is done, remove it from the grill and let it rest for a few minutes before slicing.
9. To serve, divide the herb salad among plates and top with sliced grilled chicken breasts.
10. Garnish with additional fresh herbs if desired, and serve immediately.

Enjoy your delicious grilled chicken breast with herb salad!

Mediterranean Chickpea Salad

Ingredients:

For the salad:

- 2 cans (15 ounces each) chickpeas (garbanzo beans), drained and rinsed
- 1 English cucumber, diced
- 1 pint cherry tomatoes, halved
- 1/2 red onion, thinly sliced
- 1/2 cup Kalamata olives, pitted and sliced
- 1/2 cup crumbled feta cheese
- 1/4 cup chopped fresh parsley
- 1/4 cup chopped fresh mint leaves (optional)

For the dressing:

- 1/4 cup extra virgin olive oil
- 2 tablespoons red wine vinegar
- 1 clove garlic, minced
- 1 teaspoon dried oregano
- Salt and pepper to taste

Instructions:

1. In a large mixing bowl, combine the chickpeas, diced cucumber, cherry tomatoes, red onion, Kalamata olives, crumbled feta cheese, chopped parsley, and chopped mint leaves (if using). Toss gently to combine.
2. In a small bowl, whisk together the extra virgin olive oil, red wine vinegar, minced garlic, dried oregano, salt, and pepper to create the dressing.
3. Pour the dressing over the chickpea salad and toss until everything is evenly coated.
4. Taste the salad and adjust the seasoning, if needed, by adding more salt and pepper to taste.
5. Cover the salad with plastic wrap or a lid and refrigerate for at least 30 minutes to allow the flavors to meld together.
6. Before serving, give the salad a final toss to redistribute the dressing. If desired, garnish with additional chopped parsley or mint leaves.

7. Serve the Mediterranean chickpea salad chilled as a side dish or a light main course. It's perfect for picnics, potlucks, or as a healthy lunch option.

Enjoy your delicious and flavorful Mediterranean chickpea salad!

Spinach and Feta Turkey Burgers

Ingredients:

- 1 lb ground turkey
- 2 cups fresh spinach leaves, chopped
- 1/2 cup crumbled feta cheese
- 1/4 cup finely chopped red onion
- 2 cloves garlic, minced
- 1 tablespoon Worcestershire sauce
- 1 teaspoon dried oregano
- 1/2 teaspoon salt
- 1/4 teaspoon black pepper
- Olive oil, for cooking
- Hamburger buns
- Optional toppings: lettuce, tomato, sliced red onion, avocado, tzatziki sauce

Instructions:

1. In a large mixing bowl, combine the ground turkey, chopped spinach, crumbled feta cheese, chopped red onion, minced garlic, Worcestershire sauce, dried oregano, salt, and black pepper. Use your hands or a spoon to mix everything together until well combined.
2. Divide the turkey mixture into 4 equal portions and shape each portion into a burger patty, about 1/2 to 3/4 inch thick. Press the center of each patty slightly to create an indentation; this will help the burgers cook evenly and prevent them from puffing up too much during cooking.
3. Heat a drizzle of olive oil in a skillet or grill pan over medium heat. Once hot, add the turkey burger patties to the skillet, cooking in batches if necessary to avoid overcrowding the pan.
4. Cook the turkey burgers for 5-6 minutes on each side, or until they are cooked through and no longer pink in the center. The internal temperature should reach 165°F (75°C) when measured with a meat thermometer.
5. While the burgers are cooking, you can lightly toast the hamburger buns if desired.
6. Once the turkey burgers are done, remove them from the skillet and let them rest for a few minutes before serving.

7. Assemble the burgers by placing each turkey patty on a hamburger bun and adding your desired toppings, such as lettuce, tomato, sliced red onion, avocado, and tzatziki sauce.
8. Serve the spinach and feta turkey burgers immediately, and enjoy!

These turkey burgers are flavorful, juicy, and packed with nutritious ingredients. They're sure to be a hit at your next barbecue or weeknight dinner!

Roasted Vegetable and Lentil Salad

Ingredients:

For the roasted vegetables:

- 2 cups mixed vegetables (such as bell peppers, zucchini, eggplant, cherry tomatoes, and red onion), chopped into bite-sized pieces
- 2 tablespoons olive oil
- 1 teaspoon dried thyme
- 1 teaspoon dried rosemary
- Salt and pepper to taste

For the lentils:

- 1 cup dried green or brown lentils
- 3 cups water or vegetable broth
- 2 bay leaves
- Salt to taste

For the salad:

- 4 cups mixed salad greens (such as spinach, arugula, or kale)
- 1/4 cup crumbled feta cheese (optional)
- 1/4 cup chopped fresh parsley
- 2 tablespoons lemon juice
- 2 tablespoons extra virgin olive oil
- Salt and pepper to taste

Instructions:

1. Preheat your oven to 400°F (200°C).
2. In a large mixing bowl, toss the chopped mixed vegetables with olive oil, dried thyme, dried rosemary, salt, and pepper until evenly coated.
3. Spread the seasoned vegetables in a single layer on a baking sheet lined with parchment paper or aluminum foil.
4. Roast the vegetables in the preheated oven for 20-25 minutes, or until they are tender and slightly caramelized, stirring halfway through cooking. Remove from the oven and set aside.

5. While the vegetables are roasting, rinse the lentils under cold water and drain them.
6. In a medium saucepan, combine the rinsed lentils, water or vegetable broth, and bay leaves. Bring to a boil over high heat, then reduce the heat to low and simmer, partially covered, for 20-25 minutes, or until the lentils are tender but still hold their shape. Add salt to taste during the last 10 minutes of cooking. Once done, drain any excess liquid and discard the bay leaves.
7. In a large salad bowl, combine the cooked lentils, roasted vegetables, mixed salad greens, crumbled feta cheese (if using), and chopped fresh parsley.
8. In a small bowl, whisk together the lemon juice, extra virgin olive oil, salt, and pepper to create a simple dressing.
9. Pour the dressing over the salad and toss gently to combine, making sure everything is evenly coated.
10. Taste the salad and adjust the seasoning if needed.
11. Serve the roasted vegetable and lentil salad immediately as a main course or a side dish, and enjoy!

This salad is delicious served warm or at room temperature. It's packed with fiber, protein, and vitamins, making it a wholesome and satisfying meal option.

Lemon Garlic Shrimp with Zucchini Noodles

Ingredients:

- 1 lb large shrimp, peeled and deveined
- 3 medium zucchini, spiralized into noodles
- 3 cloves garlic, minced
- Zest of 1 lemon
- Juice of 1 lemon
- 2 tablespoons olive oil
- Salt and pepper to taste
- Red pepper flakes (optional)
- Fresh parsley, chopped, for garnish

Instructions:

1. Heat 1 tablespoon of olive oil in a large skillet over medium-high heat. Add the minced garlic and cook for about 30 seconds, or until fragrant.
2. Add the shrimp to the skillet in a single layer. Season with salt, pepper, and red pepper flakes if using. Cook the shrimp for 2-3 minutes on each side, or until they are pink and opaque. Be careful not to overcook them, as they can become rubbery.
3. Once the shrimp are cooked, remove them from the skillet and set aside.
4. In the same skillet, add the remaining tablespoon of olive oil. Add the spiralized zucchini noodles to the skillet and toss them gently in the olive oil. Cook for 2-3 minutes, or until the zucchini noodles are just tender but still crisp.
5. Return the cooked shrimp to the skillet with the zucchini noodles. Add the lemon zest and lemon juice to the skillet and toss everything together to combine. Cook for an additional minute to heat everything through.
6. Taste the dish and adjust the seasoning if needed, adding more salt, pepper, or lemon juice to taste.
7. Once everything is heated through and well combined, remove the skillet from the heat.
8. Serve the lemon garlic shrimp with zucchini noodles immediately, garnished with chopped fresh parsley.

Enjoy your delicious and healthy meal of lemon garlic shrimp with zucchini noodles!

Baked Cod with Tomatoes and Olives

Ingredients:

- 4 cod fillets (about 6 ounces each)
- Salt and pepper to taste
- 2 tablespoons olive oil
- 2 cloves garlic, minced
- 1 pint cherry tomatoes, halved
- 1/2 cup Kalamata olives, pitted and sliced
- 2 tablespoons capers, drained
- 1 tablespoon fresh lemon juice
- 1 teaspoon dried oregano
- 1/4 cup chopped fresh parsley
- Lemon wedges for serving

Instructions:

1. Preheat your oven to 375°F (190°C). Grease a baking dish with olive oil or cooking spray.
2. Season the cod fillets with salt and pepper on both sides. Place them in the prepared baking dish.
3. In a skillet, heat the olive oil over medium heat. Add the minced garlic and cook for 1-2 minutes, or until fragrant.
4. Add the cherry tomatoes, Kalamata olives, and capers to the skillet. Cook for 3-4 minutes, or until the tomatoes start to soften and release their juices.
5. Stir in the fresh lemon juice and dried oregano. Cook for another minute, then remove the skillet from the heat.
6. Spoon the tomato and olive mixture evenly over the cod fillets in the baking dish.
7. Cover the baking dish with aluminum foil and bake in the preheated oven for 15-20 minutes, or until the cod is cooked through and flakes easily with a fork.
8. Once the cod is done, remove the foil from the baking dish and sprinkle the chopped fresh parsley over the top.
9. Serve the baked cod with tomatoes and olives hot, garnished with lemon wedges on the side.

Enjoy your delicious and flavorful baked cod with tomatoes and olives!

Turkey and Vegetable Stir-Fry

Ingredients:

- 1 lb turkey breast or thigh meat, thinly sliced
- 2 tablespoons soy sauce (or tamari for gluten-free)
- 2 tablespoons oyster sauce
- 1 tablespoon rice vinegar
- 1 tablespoon cornstarch
- 1 tablespoon sesame oil
- 2 tablespoons vegetable oil, divided
- 3 cloves garlic, minced
- 1 tablespoon fresh ginger, minced
- 1 onion, thinly sliced
- 2 bell peppers, thinly sliced
- 2 cups broccoli florets
- 1 cup snap peas
- Salt and pepper to taste
- Cooked rice or noodles, for serving

Instructions:

1. In a small bowl, whisk together the soy sauce, oyster sauce, rice vinegar, cornstarch, and sesame oil. Set aside.
2. Heat 1 tablespoon of vegetable oil in a large skillet or wok over medium-high heat.
3. Add the thinly sliced turkey to the skillet and cook for 2-3 minutes, stirring occasionally, until the turkey is browned and cooked through. Remove the turkey from the skillet and set it aside.
4. In the same skillet, heat the remaining tablespoon of vegetable oil over medium-high heat.
5. Add the minced garlic and ginger to the skillet and cook for about 30 seconds, until fragrant.
6. Add the thinly sliced onion, bell peppers, broccoli florets, and snap peas to the skillet. Stir-fry the vegetables for 3-4 minutes, or until they are crisp-tender.
7. Return the cooked turkey to the skillet with the vegetables.
8. Pour the sauce mixture over the turkey and vegetables in the skillet. Stir well to coat everything evenly.

9. Cook for an additional 1-2 minutes, or until the sauce has thickened and everything is heated through.
10. Taste and adjust the seasoning with salt and pepper if needed.
11. Serve the turkey and vegetable stir-fry hot over cooked rice or noodles.

Enjoy your delicious and nutritious turkey and vegetable stir-fry! Feel free to customize it with your favorite vegetables or add extra toppings like toasted sesame seeds or chopped green onions.

Caprese Stuffed Avocados

Ingredients:

- 2 ripe avocados
- 1 cup cherry or grape tomatoes, halved
- 1 cup fresh mozzarella balls (bocconcini), halved or quartered
- 1/4 cup fresh basil leaves, thinly sliced
- Balsamic glaze, for drizzling (optional)
- Extra virgin olive oil, for drizzling
- Salt and pepper to taste

Instructions:

1. Cut the avocados in half lengthwise and remove the pits. Scoop out a little extra flesh from each avocado half to create more space for the filling, if desired.
2. In a mixing bowl, combine the halved cherry tomatoes, mozzarella balls, and thinly sliced basil leaves.
3. Drizzle the tomato, mozzarella, and basil mixture with a little extra virgin olive oil. Season with salt and pepper to taste, and gently toss everything together until well combined.
4. Spoon the tomato, mozzarella, and basil mixture into the hollowed-out avocado halves, dividing it evenly among them.
5. If desired, drizzle a little balsamic glaze over the stuffed avocados for extra flavor.
6. Serve the caprese stuffed avocados immediately as a light meal or appetizer.

These caprese stuffed avocados are not only delicious but also visually appealing with their vibrant colors. They're perfect for summer gatherings or any time you're craving a fresh and healthy snack!

Kale and White Bean Soup

Ingredients:

- 2 tablespoons olive oil
- 1 onion, chopped
- 2 carrots, diced
- 2 celery stalks, diced
- 3 cloves garlic, minced
- 1 teaspoon dried thyme
- 1 teaspoon dried oregano
- 1/2 teaspoon smoked paprika
- 6 cups vegetable broth or chicken broth
- 2 (15-ounce) cans white beans (such as cannellini or Great Northern), drained and rinsed
- 1 bunch kale, stems removed and leaves chopped
- Salt and pepper to taste
- Juice of 1 lemon
- Grated Parmesan cheese for serving (optional)

Instructions:

1. In a large pot or Dutch oven, heat the olive oil over medium heat. Add the chopped onion, diced carrots, and diced celery. Cook, stirring occasionally, for 5-6 minutes, or until the vegetables start to soften.
2. Add the minced garlic, dried thyme, dried oregano, and smoked paprika to the pot. Cook for another 1-2 minutes, or until the garlic is fragrant.
3. Pour in the vegetable broth or chicken broth, and bring the soup to a simmer.
4. Once the soup is simmering, add the drained and rinsed white beans to the pot. Stir well to combine.
5. Add the chopped kale to the pot, stirring it into the soup. Cook for 5-7 minutes, or until the kale is wilted and tender.
6. Season the soup with salt and pepper to taste. Adjust the seasoning as needed.
7. Stir in the lemon juice, then taste the soup and adjust the acidity with more lemon juice if desired.
8. Ladle the kale and white bean soup into bowls and serve hot.
9. If desired, garnish each serving with grated Parmesan cheese.

Enjoy your delicious and hearty kale and white bean soup! It's full of flavor, packed with nutrients, and sure to warm you up from the inside out.

Grilled Vegetable Skewers

Ingredients:

- Assorted vegetables (such as bell peppers, zucchini, yellow squash, red onion, cherry tomatoes, mushrooms, and eggplant)
- Olive oil
- Balsamic vinegar (optional)
- Garlic powder
- Dried herbs (such as oregano, thyme, or rosemary)
- Salt and pepper to taste
- Wooden or metal skewers

Instructions:

1. If using wooden skewers, soak them in water for at least 30 minutes before grilling to prevent them from burning.
2. Prepare the vegetables by washing them and cutting them into bite-sized pieces. Try to cut them into uniform sizes so they cook evenly on the grill.
3. Place the cut vegetables in a large mixing bowl. Drizzle them with olive oil and balsamic vinegar (if using), and sprinkle with garlic powder, dried herbs, salt, and pepper. Toss the vegetables until they are evenly coated with the seasonings.
4. Thread the seasoned vegetables onto the skewers, alternating the different types of vegetables to create colorful and varied skewers.
5. Preheat your grill to medium-high heat.
6. Once the grill is hot, place the vegetable skewers on the grill grates. Cook for 8-10 minutes, turning occasionally, or until the vegetables are tender and lightly charred.
7. Remove the grilled vegetable skewers from the grill and transfer them to a serving platter.
8. Serve the grilled vegetable skewers hot as a side dish or appetizer at your barbecue or outdoor gathering.

These grilled vegetable skewers are versatile and customizable, so feel free to use your favorite vegetables and seasonings. They're perfect for vegetarians and meat lovers alike, and they add a burst of color and flavor to any meal!

Herb-Roasted Chicken Thighs

Ingredients:

- 8 bone-in, skin-on chicken thighs
- 2 tablespoons olive oil
- 3 cloves garlic, minced
- 1 tablespoon chopped fresh rosemary
- 1 tablespoon chopped fresh thyme
- 1 tablespoon chopped fresh parsley
- 1 teaspoon dried oregano
- 1 teaspoon dried basil
- Salt and pepper to taste
- Lemon wedges for serving (optional)

Instructions:

1. Preheat your oven to 400°F (200°C). Line a baking sheet with parchment paper or aluminum foil for easy cleanup.
2. In a small bowl, combine the olive oil, minced garlic, chopped fresh rosemary, thyme, parsley, dried oregano, dried basil, salt, and pepper to create a herb-infused marinade.
3. Pat the chicken thighs dry with paper towels and place them on the prepared baking sheet.
4. Rub the herb-infused marinade all over the chicken thighs, making sure they are evenly coated on all sides.
5. Arrange the chicken thighs skin-side up on the baking sheet, leaving a little space between each piece.
6. Roast the chicken thighs in the preheated oven for 35-40 minutes, or until they are golden brown and cooked through. The internal temperature of the chicken should reach 165°F (75°C) when measured with a meat thermometer.
7. Once the chicken thighs are done, remove them from the oven and let them rest for a few minutes before serving.
8. Serve the herb-roasted chicken thighs hot with lemon wedges on the side for squeezing over the chicken, if desired.

These herb-roasted chicken thighs are delicious served with roasted vegetables, mashed potatoes, or a simple green salad. They're perfect for a family dinner or entertaining guests, and the aroma of the herbs will fill your kitchen with irresistible fragrance!

Cauliflower Rice Stir-Fry

Ingredients:

For the cauliflower rice:

- 1 large head of cauliflower
- 2 tablespoons olive oil
- 2 cloves garlic, minced
- Salt and pepper to taste

For the stir-fry:

- 2 tablespoons sesame oil
- 1 onion, thinly sliced
- 2 carrots, julienned
- 1 bell pepper, thinly sliced
- 1 cup broccoli florets
- 1 cup snap peas
- 1 cup sliced mushrooms
- 3 tablespoons soy sauce (or tamari for gluten-free)
- 2 tablespoons hoisin sauce
- 1 tablespoon rice vinegar
- 1 teaspoon grated ginger
- Optional toppings: sliced green onions, sesame seeds, chopped cilantro

Instructions:

1. Prepare the cauliflower rice: Cut the cauliflower into florets and place them in a food processor. Pulse until the cauliflower resembles rice-like grains.
2. Heat 2 tablespoons of olive oil in a large skillet or wok over medium heat. Add the minced garlic and cook for about 1 minute, until fragrant.
3. Add the cauliflower rice to the skillet and season with salt and pepper. Stir-fry for about 5-7 minutes, until the cauliflower is tender but not mushy. Transfer the cauliflower rice to a plate and set aside.

4. In the same skillet or wok, heat 2 tablespoons of sesame oil over medium-high heat. Add the thinly sliced onion and julienned carrots. Stir-fry for 2-3 minutes, until the vegetables start to soften.
5. Add the thinly sliced bell pepper, broccoli florets, snap peas, and sliced mushrooms to the skillet. Continue to stir-fry for another 3-4 minutes, until all the vegetables are tender-crisp.
6. In a small bowl, whisk together the soy sauce, hoisin sauce, rice vinegar, and grated ginger to create the stir-fry sauce.
7. Pour the stir-fry sauce over the vegetables in the skillet. Stir well to coat everything evenly and cook for another 1-2 minutes, until the sauce thickens slightly.
8. Add the cooked cauliflower rice back to the skillet with the stir-fried vegetables. Stir everything together until well combined and heated through.
9. Taste the stir-fry and adjust the seasoning if needed.
10. Serve the cauliflower rice stir-fry hot, garnished with sliced green onions, sesame seeds, and chopped cilantro if desired.

Enjoy your delicious and healthy cauliflower rice stir-fry! It's packed with flavor and nutrients, making it a satisfying meal for any day of the week.

Tuna and White Bean Salad

Ingredients:

- 2 cans (5 ounces each) tuna in water, drained
- 2 cans (15 ounces each) white beans (such as cannellini or Great Northern), drained and rinsed
- 1/2 red onion, finely diced
- 1/4 cup chopped fresh parsley
- 2 tablespoons capers, drained (optional)
- 2 tablespoons extra virgin olive oil
- 2 tablespoons lemon juice
- Salt and pepper to taste

Instructions:

1. In a large mixing bowl, combine the drained tuna, white beans, finely diced red onion, chopped fresh parsley, and drained capers (if using).
2. In a small bowl, whisk together the extra virgin olive oil and lemon juice to create a simple dressing.
3. Pour the dressing over the tuna and white bean mixture in the large bowl.
4. Gently toss everything together until well combined and evenly coated with the dressing.
5. Season the salad with salt and pepper to taste, adjusting the seasoning as needed.
6. Serve the tuna and white bean salad immediately, or chill it in the refrigerator for at least 30 minutes to allow the flavors to meld together before serving.
7. Enjoy your delicious and nutritious tuna and white bean salad as a light meal or side dish. It's perfect for lunch, picnics, or as a protein-packed snack!

Feel free to customize this recipe by adding other ingredients such as chopped celery, cherry tomatoes, or olives, or by incorporating different herbs and spices to suit your taste preferences.

Stuffed Portobello Mushrooms with Spinach and Feta

Ingredients:

- 4 large portobello mushrooms
- 2 tablespoons olive oil
- 2 cloves garlic, minced
- 4 cups fresh spinach leaves, chopped
- 1/2 cup crumbled feta cheese
- 1/4 cup grated Parmesan cheese
- Salt and pepper to taste
- Optional: red pepper flakes for added heat

Instructions:

1. Preheat your oven to 375°F (190°C). Line a baking sheet with parchment paper or foil for easy cleanup.
2. Clean the portobello mushrooms by gently wiping them with a damp paper towel to remove any dirt. Remove the stems and use a spoon to scrape out the gills from the underside of the mushrooms.
3. In a large skillet, heat the olive oil over medium heat. Add the minced garlic and cook for about 1 minute, until fragrant.
4. Add the chopped spinach to the skillet and cook, stirring occasionally, until wilted, about 2-3 minutes. Season with salt, pepper, and red pepper flakes (if using).
5. Remove the skillet from the heat and stir in the crumbled feta cheese until well combined.
6. Place the portobello mushrooms on the prepared baking sheet, gill side up. Divide the spinach and feta mixture evenly among the mushrooms, filling each cap.
7. Sprinkle the grated Parmesan cheese over the stuffed mushrooms.
8. Bake in the preheated oven for 15-20 minutes, or until the mushrooms are tender and the cheese is melted and golden brown on top.
9. Once done, remove the stuffed portobello mushrooms from the oven and let them cool for a few minutes before serving.
10. Serve the stuffed portobello mushrooms as a delicious appetizer or as a main course alongside a fresh salad or crusty bread.

Enjoy your flavorful stuffed portobello mushrooms with spinach and feta! They're perfect for a meatless meal option that's both satisfying and packed with nutrients.

Greek Chicken Souvlaki with Tzatziki Sauce

Ingredients:

For the chicken souvlaki:

- 1.5 lbs boneless, skinless chicken breasts or thighs, cut into bite-sized pieces
- 1/4 cup olive oil
- 3 cloves garlic, minced
- Juice of 1 lemon
- 1 teaspoon dried oregano
- 1 teaspoon dried thyme
- 1 teaspoon dried rosemary
- Salt and pepper to taste
- Wooden skewers, soaked in water for at least 30 minutes

For the tzatziki sauce:

- 1 cup Greek yogurt
- 1 cucumber, grated and squeezed to remove excess moisture
- 2 cloves garlic, minced
- 1 tablespoon extra virgin olive oil
- 1 tablespoon lemon juice
- 1 tablespoon chopped fresh dill (or 1 teaspoon dried dill)
- Salt and pepper to taste

For serving:

- Pita bread or flatbread
- Sliced tomatoes
- Sliced red onion
- Chopped fresh parsley or cilantro for garnish (optional)
- Lemon wedges for serving

Instructions:

1. In a bowl, combine the olive oil, minced garlic, lemon juice, dried oregano, dried thyme, dried rosemary, salt, and pepper to create a marinade for the chicken.

2. Add the chicken pieces to the marinade and toss until well coated. Cover and refrigerate for at least 30 minutes, or up to 4 hours, to allow the flavors to meld together.
3. While the chicken is marinating, prepare the tzatziki sauce. In a mixing bowl, combine the Greek yogurt, grated cucumber, minced garlic, extra virgin olive oil, lemon juice, chopped fresh dill, salt, and pepper. Stir until well combined. Cover and refrigerate until ready to serve.
4. Preheat your grill to medium-high heat.
5. Thread the marinated chicken pieces onto the soaked wooden skewers, dividing them evenly among the skewers.
6. Grill the chicken skewers for 8-10 minutes, turning occasionally, or until the chicken is cooked through and has nice grill marks.
7. While the chicken is grilling, warm the pita bread or flatbread on the grill for a minute or two on each side.
8. Once the chicken is done, remove the skewers from the grill and let them rest for a few minutes.
9. To serve, place a few chicken skewers on each warmed pita bread or flatbread. Top with sliced tomatoes, sliced red onion, and a generous dollop of tzatziki sauce. Sprinkle with chopped fresh parsley or cilantro if desired. Serve with lemon wedges on the side.
10. Enjoy your delicious Greek chicken souvlaki with tzatziki sauce as a satisfying meal!

Lentil and Vegetable Curry

Ingredients:

- 1 cup dried green or brown lentils, rinsed and drained
- 2 tablespoons olive oil
- 1 onion, chopped
- 3 cloves garlic, minced
- 1 tablespoon grated ginger
- 2 carrots, diced
- 2 potatoes, diced
- 1 bell pepper, diced
- 1 zucchini, diced
- 1 can (14 ounces) diced tomatoes
- 1 can (14 ounces) coconut milk
- 2 cups vegetable broth
- 2 tablespoons curry powder
- 1 teaspoon ground cumin
- 1 teaspoon ground coriander
- 1/2 teaspoon turmeric powder
- Salt and pepper to taste
- Fresh cilantro, chopped, for garnish (optional)
- Cooked rice or naan bread, for serving

Instructions:

1. Heat the olive oil in a large pot or Dutch oven over medium heat. Add the chopped onion and cook until softened, about 5 minutes.
2. Add the minced garlic and grated ginger to the pot, and cook for another minute, until fragrant.
3. Stir in the diced carrots, potatoes, bell pepper, and zucchini. Cook for 5-7 minutes, stirring occasionally, until the vegetables start to soften.
4. Add the rinsed lentils, diced tomatoes (with their juices), coconut milk, vegetable broth, curry powder, ground cumin, ground coriander, turmeric powder, salt, and pepper to the pot. Stir everything together until well combined.
5. Bring the mixture to a simmer, then reduce the heat to low. Cover and cook for 25-30 minutes, or until the lentils and vegetables are tender, stirring occasionally.
6. Taste the curry and adjust the seasoning with more salt and pepper if needed.

7. Once the lentil and vegetable curry is done cooking, remove it from the heat and let it sit for a few minutes to allow the flavors to meld together.
8. Serve the curry hot over cooked rice or with naan bread. Garnish with fresh chopped cilantro if desired.
9. Enjoy your delicious and nutritious lentil and vegetable curry as a comforting and satisfying meal!

This curry is versatile, so feel free to customize it by adding other vegetables or adjusting the spices to suit your taste preferences. It's perfect for meal prep and makes great leftovers for lunch the next day!

Lemon Herb Grilled Tilapia

Ingredients:

- 4 tilapia fillets
- Zest and juice of 1 lemon
- 2 tablespoons olive oil
- 2 cloves garlic, minced
- 1 teaspoon dried thyme
- 1 teaspoon dried rosemary
- Salt and pepper to taste
- Fresh parsley, chopped, for garnish (optional)
- Lemon wedges for serving

Instructions:

1. In a small bowl, whisk together the lemon zest, lemon juice, olive oil, minced garlic, dried thyme, dried rosemary, salt, and pepper to create a marinade.
2. Place the tilapia fillets in a shallow dish or resealable plastic bag. Pour the marinade over the tilapia, making sure to coat each fillet evenly. Cover the dish or seal the bag and refrigerate for at least 30 minutes, or up to 2 hours, to allow the flavors to meld together.
3. Preheat your grill to medium-high heat. Lightly oil the grill grates to prevent the fish from sticking.
4. Remove the tilapia fillets from the marinade and discard any excess marinade.
5. Place the tilapia fillets on the preheated grill. Grill for 3-4 minutes on each side, or until the fish is opaque and flakes easily with a fork.
6. Once the tilapia is done cooking, remove it from the grill and transfer it to a serving platter.
7. Garnish the grilled tilapia with chopped fresh parsley, if desired, and serve hot with lemon wedges on the side.
8. Enjoy your delicious and flavorful lemon herb grilled tilapia as a light and healthy main course!

This grilled tilapia pairs well with a variety of side dishes, such as steamed vegetables, rice, or a fresh salad. It's perfect for a summer barbecue or a quick weeknight dinner option.

Turkey and Quinoa Meatballs

Ingredients:

- 1 lb ground turkey (preferably lean)
- 1 cup cooked quinoa
- 1/4 cup grated Parmesan cheese
- 1/4 cup finely chopped onion
- 2 cloves garlic, minced
- 1/4 cup chopped fresh parsley
- 1 teaspoon dried oregano
- 1 teaspoon dried basil
- 1/2 teaspoon salt
- 1/4 teaspoon black pepper
- 1 large egg, lightly beaten
- Olive oil, for greasing baking sheet

Instructions:

1. Preheat your oven to 375°F (190°C). Grease a baking sheet with olive oil or line it with parchment paper.
2. In a large mixing bowl, combine the ground turkey, cooked quinoa, grated Parmesan cheese, finely chopped onion, minced garlic, chopped fresh parsley, dried oregano, dried basil, salt, black pepper, and beaten egg. Mix everything together until well combined.
3. Shape the mixture into meatballs, using about 1-2 tablespoons of the mixture for each meatball. Roll the mixture between your palms to form evenly sized meatballs.
4. Place the meatballs on the prepared baking sheet, leaving a little space between each one.
5. Bake the meatballs in the preheated oven for 20-25 minutes, or until they are cooked through and lightly browned on the outside.
6. Once the meatballs are done baking, remove them from the oven and let them cool for a few minutes before serving.
7. Serve the turkey and quinoa meatballs hot as a main course or appetizer. You can enjoy them on their own, with your favorite sauce, or as part of a pasta dish or sandwich.
8. Store any leftovers in an airtight container in the refrigerator for up to 3-4 days, or freeze them for longer storage.

These turkey and quinoa meatballs are delicious, nutritious, and versatile. They're a great option for meal prep and can be enjoyed in a variety of ways throughout the week!

Greek Salad with Grilled Chicken

Ingredients:

For the Greek salad:

- 2 large tomatoes, diced
- 1 cucumber, diced
- 1 red bell pepper, diced
- 1/2 red onion, thinly sliced
- 1/2 cup Kalamata olives, pitted
- 1/2 cup crumbled feta cheese
- 1/4 cup chopped fresh parsley
- 2 tablespoons extra virgin olive oil
- 1 tablespoon red wine vinegar
- Salt and pepper to taste
- Optional: 1/2 teaspoon dried oregano

For the grilled chicken:

- 2 boneless, skinless chicken breasts
- 2 tablespoons olive oil
- 2 cloves garlic, minced
- Juice of 1 lemon
- 1 teaspoon dried oregano
- Salt and pepper to taste

Instructions:

1. In a large mixing bowl, combine the diced tomatoes, diced cucumber, diced red bell pepper, thinly sliced red onion, pitted Kalamata olives, crumbled feta cheese, and chopped fresh parsley to make the Greek salad.
2. In a small bowl, whisk together the extra virgin olive oil, red wine vinegar, salt, pepper, and dried oregano (if using) to create the dressing for the Greek salad.
3. Pour the dressing over the salad ingredients in the large mixing bowl. Toss everything together until well combined. Set aside while you prepare the grilled chicken.
4. Preheat your grill to medium-high heat.

5. In a bowl, combine the olive oil, minced garlic, lemon juice, dried oregano, salt, and pepper to create a marinade for the chicken breasts.
6. Place the chicken breasts in the marinade and toss until well coated. Let the chicken marinate for 15-30 minutes while the grill heats up.
7. Once the grill is hot, grill the chicken breasts for 6-8 minutes on each side, or until they are cooked through and have nice grill marks. The internal temperature of the chicken should reach 165°F (75°C) when measured with a meat thermometer.
8. Remove the grilled chicken breasts from the grill and let them rest for a few minutes before slicing.
9. To serve, divide the Greek salad among serving plates or bowls. Top each serving with sliced grilled chicken.
10. Serve the Greek salad with grilled chicken immediately, and enjoy!

This Greek salad with grilled chicken is perfect for a light and healthy lunch or dinner. It's full of fresh flavors and makes a satisfying meal on its own. Feel free to customize the salad with your favorite vegetables or add extras like avocado or chickpeas for added protein and texture.

Ratatouille with Herbed Quinoa

Ingredients:

For the ratatouille:

- 1 large eggplant, diced
- 2 zucchini, diced
- 1 yellow squash, diced
- 1 red bell pepper, diced
- 1 yellow bell pepper, diced
- 1 onion, diced
- 3 cloves garlic, minced
- 2 cups diced tomatoes (fresh or canned)
- 2 tablespoons tomato paste
- 2 tablespoons extra virgin olive oil
- 1 teaspoon dried thyme
- 1 teaspoon dried oregano
- Salt and pepper to taste
- Fresh basil leaves, chopped, for garnish

For the herbed quinoa:

- 1 cup quinoa, rinsed
- 2 cups vegetable broth or water
- 2 tablespoons chopped fresh parsley
- 1 tablespoon chopped fresh basil
- 1 tablespoon chopped fresh thyme
- Salt and pepper to taste

Instructions:

1. Preheat your oven to 375°F (190°C).
2. In a large mixing bowl, combine the diced eggplant, diced zucchini, diced yellow squash, diced red bell pepper, diced yellow bell pepper, diced onion, minced garlic, diced tomatoes, tomato paste, extra virgin olive oil, dried thyme, dried

oregano, salt, and pepper to make the ratatouille mixture. Toss everything together until well combined.
3. Transfer the ratatouille mixture to a large baking dish or roasting pan, spreading it out into an even layer.
4. Cover the baking dish or roasting pan with foil and bake in the preheated oven for 45-50 minutes, or until the vegetables are tender and cooked through.
5. While the ratatouille is baking, prepare the herbed quinoa. In a medium saucepan, combine the rinsed quinoa and vegetable broth or water. Bring to a boil, then reduce the heat to low, cover, and simmer for 15-20 minutes, or until the quinoa is cooked and the liquid is absorbed.
6. Once the quinoa is cooked, fluff it with a fork and stir in the chopped fresh parsley, chopped fresh basil, chopped fresh thyme, salt, and pepper.
7. When the ratatouille is done baking, remove it from the oven and let it cool for a few minutes.
8. Serve the ratatouille warm over the herbed quinoa, garnished with chopped fresh basil leaves.
9. Enjoy your delicious ratatouille with herbed quinoa as a flavorful and satisfying vegetarian meal!

This dish is full of vibrant flavors and textures, making it perfect for a healthy lunch or dinner. Plus, it's packed with nutritious vegetables and protein-rich quinoa, making it a well-balanced meal. Feel free to customize the recipe with your favorite herbs and vegetables to suit your taste preferences.

Baked Sweet Potatoes with Black Bean Salsa

Ingredients:

For the baked sweet potatoes:

- 4 medium sweet potatoes
- 2 tablespoons olive oil
- Salt and pepper to taste

For the black bean salsa:

- 1 can (15 ounces) black beans, drained and rinsed
- 1 cup diced tomatoes
- 1/2 cup diced red onion
- 1/2 cup diced bell pepper (any color)
- 1/4 cup chopped fresh cilantro
- 1 jalapeño pepper, seeded and minced (optional)
- Juice of 1 lime
- 2 tablespoons olive oil
- 1 teaspoon ground cumin
- Salt and pepper to taste

Instructions:

1. Preheat your oven to 400°F (200°C). Line a baking sheet with parchment paper or aluminum foil.
2. Scrub the sweet potatoes under cold water to clean them. Pat them dry with paper towels.
3. Pierce each sweet potato several times with a fork to allow steam to escape during baking.
4. Place the sweet potatoes on the prepared baking sheet. Drizzle each sweet potato with olive oil and season with salt and pepper.
5. Bake the sweet potatoes in the preheated oven for 45-60 minutes, or until they are tender and easily pierced with a fork.
6. While the sweet potatoes are baking, prepare the black bean salsa. In a large mixing bowl, combine the black beans, diced tomatoes, diced red onion, diced

bell pepper, chopped fresh cilantro, minced jalapeño pepper (if using), lime juice, olive oil, ground cumin, salt, and pepper. Mix well to combine.
7. Once the sweet potatoes are done baking, remove them from the oven and let them cool for a few minutes.
8. To serve, slice each sweet potato lengthwise and slightly mash the flesh with a fork. Top each sweet potato with a generous scoop of black bean salsa.
9. Garnish with additional chopped cilantro, if desired, and serve immediately.
10. Enjoy your delicious baked sweet potatoes with black bean salsa as a nutritious and flavorful meal!

This dish is not only tasty but also packed with protein, fiber, vitamins, and minerals. It's perfect for a healthy lunch or dinner option and can be easily customized with your favorite toppings or additional spices.

Spicy Garlic Shrimp with Brown Rice

Ingredients:

For the spicy garlic shrimp:

- 1 lb large shrimp, peeled and deveined
- 3 tablespoons olive oil
- 4 cloves garlic, minced
- 1 teaspoon red pepper flakes (adjust to taste)
- 1 teaspoon paprika
- Salt and pepper to taste
- 2 tablespoons chopped fresh parsley
- 1 tablespoon lemon juice

For the brown rice:

- 1 cup brown rice
- 2 cups water or vegetable broth
- Salt to taste

Instructions:

1. Rinse the brown rice under cold water until the water runs clear. This helps remove excess starch.
2. In a medium saucepan, combine the rinsed brown rice, water or vegetable broth, and a pinch of salt. Bring to a boil over high heat.
3. Reduce the heat to low, cover, and simmer for 40-45 minutes, or until the rice is tender and the liquid is absorbed. Remove from heat and let it sit, covered, for 5 minutes. Fluff the rice with a fork before serving.
4. While the rice is cooking, prepare the spicy garlic shrimp. In a large skillet, heat the olive oil over medium heat.
5. Add the minced garlic and red pepper flakes to the skillet. Cook for 1-2 minutes, stirring constantly, until the garlic is fragrant and golden brown.
6. Add the shrimp to the skillet in a single layer. Sprinkle with paprika, salt, and pepper to taste.
7. Cook the shrimp for 2-3 minutes on each side, or until they are pink and opaque.

8. Remove the skillet from the heat and sprinkle the chopped fresh parsley over the shrimp. Drizzle with lemon juice and toss to coat evenly.
9. To serve, divide the cooked brown rice among serving plates or bowls. Top with the spicy garlic shrimp.
10. Garnish with additional chopped parsley and lemon wedges, if desired.
11. Enjoy your delicious spicy garlic shrimp with brown rice as a flavorful and nutritious meal!

This dish is versatile, so feel free to customize it by adding your favorite vegetables or adjusting the level of spiciness to suit your taste preferences. It's perfect for a quick weeknight dinner or for entertaining guests.

Mediterranean Veggie Wrap with Hummus

Ingredients:

- 4 large whole wheat or spinach tortillas
- 1 cup hummus (store-bought or homemade)
- 1 large cucumber, thinly sliced
- 1 red bell pepper, thinly sliced
- 1 yellow bell pepper, thinly sliced
- 1 cup cherry tomatoes, halved
- 1/2 red onion, thinly sliced
- 1/2 cup sliced Kalamata olives
- 1 cup mixed salad greens (such as spinach, arugula, or lettuce)
- 1/4 cup crumbled feta cheese (optional)
- 1/4 cup chopped fresh parsley or basil (optional)
- Salt and pepper to taste

Instructions:

1. Lay out the tortillas on a clean work surface.
2. Spread a generous amount of hummus over each tortilla, leaving a border around the edges.
3. Layer the sliced cucumber, red bell pepper, yellow bell pepper, cherry tomatoes, red onion, Kalamata olives, mixed salad greens, crumbled feta cheese (if using), and chopped fresh parsley or basil (if using) evenly over the hummus on each tortilla.
4. Season the veggies with salt and pepper to taste.
5. Fold in the sides of each tortilla, then roll them up tightly from the bottom to create wraps.
6. If desired, slice each wrap in half diagonally before serving.
7. Serve the Mediterranean veggie wraps with hummus immediately, or wrap them tightly in foil or parchment paper for a convenient grab-and-go meal.
8. Enjoy your delicious and nutritious Mediterranean veggie wraps with hummus!

Feel free to customize these wraps with your favorite Mediterranean-inspired ingredients, such as roasted red peppers, artichoke hearts, sun-dried tomatoes, or grilled eggplant. You can also add grilled chicken or tofu for extra protein if desired. These wraps are versatile and can be enjoyed for lunch, dinner, or as a portable snack.

Grilled Lemon Herb Chicken Skewers

Ingredients:

- 1.5 lbs boneless, skinless chicken breasts or thighs, cut into 1-inch cubes
- Zest and juice of 1 lemon
- 3 tablespoons olive oil
- 2 cloves garlic, minced
- 1 tablespoon chopped fresh parsley
- 1 tablespoon chopped fresh thyme
- 1 tablespoon chopped fresh rosemary
- 1 teaspoon dried oregano
- 1 teaspoon salt
- 1/2 teaspoon black pepper
- Wooden skewers, soaked in water for at least 30 minutes

Instructions:

1. In a large mixing bowl, combine the lemon zest, lemon juice, olive oil, minced garlic, chopped fresh parsley, chopped fresh thyme, chopped fresh rosemary, dried oregano, salt, and black pepper to create a marinade.
2. Add the chicken cubes to the marinade and toss until well coated. Cover the bowl and refrigerate for at least 30 minutes, or up to 4 hours, to allow the flavors to meld together.
3. Preheat your grill to medium-high heat.
4. Thread the marinated chicken cubes onto the soaked wooden skewers, dividing them evenly among the skewers.
5. Lightly oil the grill grates to prevent the chicken from sticking.
6. Place the chicken skewers on the preheated grill. Grill for 8-10 minutes, turning occasionally, or until the chicken is cooked through and has nice grill marks.
7. Once the chicken is done cooking, remove the skewers from the grill and let them rest for a few minutes before serving.
8. Serve the grilled lemon herb chicken skewers hot, garnished with additional chopped fresh herbs if desired.
9. Enjoy your delicious and flavorful grilled lemon herb chicken skewers as a main course or as part of a summer barbecue!

These chicken skewers are perfect for serving with your favorite side dishes, such as rice, grilled vegetables, or a fresh salad. They're also great for meal prep and can be enjoyed as leftovers for lunch or dinner the next day.

Black Bean and Corn Salad with Cilantro Lime Dressing

Ingredients:

For the salad:

- 2 cans (15 ounces each) black beans, drained and rinsed
- 2 cups frozen corn kernels, thawed
- 1 red bell pepper, diced
- 1/2 red onion, finely chopped
- 1 jalapeño pepper, seeded and finely chopped (optional, for added heat)
- 1/4 cup chopped fresh cilantro
- Salt and pepper to taste
- Optional: diced avocado, cherry tomatoes, or diced mango for additional flavor and color

For the cilantro lime dressing:

- 1/4 cup fresh lime juice (about 2-3 limes)
- 1/4 cup extra virgin olive oil
- 2 tablespoons chopped fresh cilantro
- 1 tablespoon honey or maple syrup (for sweetness)
- 1 teaspoon minced garlic
- 1/2 teaspoon ground cumin
- Salt and pepper to taste

Instructions:

1. In a large mixing bowl, combine the black beans, corn kernels, diced red bell pepper, finely chopped red onion, chopped jalapeño pepper (if using), and chopped fresh cilantro.
2. If using additional ingredients like diced avocado, cherry tomatoes, or diced mango, add them to the bowl as well.
3. Season the salad with salt and pepper to taste, and toss everything together until well combined.
4. In a small bowl or jar, whisk together the fresh lime juice, extra virgin olive oil, chopped cilantro, honey or maple syrup, minced garlic, ground cumin, salt, and pepper to create the cilantro lime dressing.
5. Pour the dressing over the salad in the large mixing bowl.

6. Toss the salad again until everything is evenly coated with the dressing.
7. Taste and adjust the seasoning as needed, adding more salt, pepper, or lime juice to suit your taste preferences.
8. Cover the bowl and refrigerate the black bean and corn salad for at least 30 minutes to allow the flavors to meld together before serving.
9. Once chilled, give the salad a final toss and serve cold.
10. Enjoy your delicious black bean and corn salad with cilantro lime dressing as a side dish or as a light and refreshing meal on its own!

This salad is versatile and can be customized with your favorite ingredients. It's perfect for meal prep and can be stored in the refrigerator for a few days, allowing you to enjoy it throughout the week.

Turkey Chili with Kidney Beans

Ingredients:

- 1 tablespoon olive oil
- 1 onion, diced
- 3 cloves garlic, minced
- 1 bell pepper, diced
- 1 lb ground turkey
- 1 can (15 ounces) kidney beans, drained and rinsed
- 1 can (15 ounces) diced tomatoes
- 1 can (6 ounces) tomato paste
- 1 cup chicken broth
- 2 tablespoons chili powder
- 1 teaspoon ground cumin
- 1 teaspoon dried oregano
- 1/2 teaspoon paprika
- Salt and pepper to taste
- Optional toppings: shredded cheese, chopped green onions, sour cream, avocado slices, chopped cilantro

Instructions:

1. In a large pot or Dutch oven, heat the olive oil over medium heat.
2. Add the diced onion, minced garlic, and diced bell pepper to the pot. Cook for 5-7 minutes, or until the vegetables are softened.
3. Add the ground turkey to the pot, breaking it up with a spoon. Cook, stirring occasionally, until the turkey is browned and cooked through.
4. Stir in the drained and rinsed kidney beans, diced tomatoes, tomato paste, chicken broth, chili powder, ground cumin, dried oregano, paprika, salt, and pepper.
5. Bring the chili to a simmer, then reduce the heat to low. Cover and let the chili cook for 20-30 minutes, stirring occasionally, to allow the flavors to meld together and the chili to thicken.
6. Taste the chili and adjust the seasoning with more salt, pepper, or chili powder if needed.
7. Once the chili is done cooking and has reached your desired consistency, remove it from the heat.

8. Serve the turkey chili hot, garnished with your favorite toppings such as shredded cheese, chopped green onions, sour cream, avocado slices, or chopped cilantro.
9. Enjoy your delicious turkey chili with kidney beans as a comforting and satisfying meal!

This turkey chili is perfect for serving on its own or alongside cornbread, rice, or tortilla chips. It's also great for meal prep and can be stored in the refrigerator for a few days or frozen for longer storage.

Balsamic Glazed Salmon with Asparagus

Ingredients:

For the balsamic glaze:

- 1/4 cup balsamic vinegar
- 2 tablespoons honey or maple syrup
- 1 tablespoon soy sauce or tamari
- 2 cloves garlic, minced
- 1 teaspoon Dijon mustard
- Salt and pepper to taste

For the salmon and asparagus:

- 4 salmon fillets, skin-on or skinless (about 6 ounces each)
- 1 bunch asparagus, woody ends trimmed
- 1 tablespoon olive oil
- Salt and pepper to taste
- Optional garnish: chopped fresh parsley or sliced green onions

Instructions:

1. Preheat your oven to 400°F (200°C). Line a baking sheet with parchment paper or aluminum foil for easy cleanup.
2. In a small saucepan, combine the balsamic vinegar, honey or maple syrup, soy sauce or tamari, minced garlic, Dijon mustard, salt, and pepper. Bring the mixture to a simmer over medium heat, then reduce the heat to low. Let it simmer for 5-7 minutes, stirring occasionally, until the glaze thickens slightly. Remove the saucepan from the heat and set aside.
3. Place the salmon fillets on the prepared baking sheet. Brush each fillet generously with the balsamic glaze, reserving some glaze for later.
4. Arrange the trimmed asparagus spears around the salmon fillets on the baking sheet. Drizzle the asparagus with olive oil and season with salt and pepper to taste.
5. Place the baking sheet in the preheated oven and bake for 12-15 minutes, or until the salmon is cooked through and flakes easily with a fork, and the asparagus is tender-crisp.

6. During the last few minutes of baking, brush the salmon fillets with any remaining balsamic glaze to add extra flavor and shine.
7. Once the salmon and asparagus are done baking, remove them from the oven and let them cool for a few minutes.
8. To serve, transfer the salmon fillets and asparagus spears to serving plates. Garnish with chopped fresh parsley or sliced green onions if desired.
9. Enjoy your delicious balsamic glazed salmon with asparagus as a nutritious and satisfying meal!

This dish pairs well with rice, quinoa, or roasted potatoes. It's perfect for a weeknight dinner or for entertaining guests. Feel free to customize the recipe by adding your favorite herbs or spices to the glaze, or by swapping out the asparagus for other vegetables like green beans or broccoli.

Roasted Brussels Sprouts with Garlic and Parmesan

Ingredients:

- 1 lb Brussels sprouts, trimmed and halved
- 2 tablespoons olive oil
- 3 cloves garlic, minced
- Salt and pepper to taste
- 1/4 cup grated Parmesan cheese
- Optional: red pepper flakes for added heat
- Optional: lemon wedges for serving

Instructions:

1. Preheat your oven to 400°F (200°C). Line a baking sheet with parchment paper or aluminum foil for easy cleanup.
2. In a large mixing bowl, toss the halved Brussels sprouts with olive oil, minced garlic, salt, and pepper until evenly coated.
3. Spread the Brussels sprouts out in a single layer on the prepared baking sheet, cut side down.
4. Roast the Brussels sprouts in the preheated oven for 20-25 minutes, or until they are tender and caramelized on the edges, stirring halfway through cooking.
5. Once the Brussels sprouts are done roasting, remove them from the oven and transfer them to a serving dish.
6. Sprinkle the roasted Brussels sprouts with grated Parmesan cheese while they are still hot, allowing the cheese to melt slightly.
7. If desired, sprinkle red pepper flakes over the Brussels sprouts for added heat.
8. Serve the roasted Brussels sprouts with garlic and Parmesan hot, with lemon wedges on the side for squeezing over the top for extra brightness.
9. Enjoy your delicious roasted Brussels sprouts with garlic and Parmesan as a tasty and nutritious side dish!

These roasted Brussels sprouts make a great accompaniment to any meal, whether it's a weeknight dinner or a holiday feast. They're packed with flavor and nutrients and are sure to be a hit with everyone at the table. Feel free to customize the recipe by adding your favorite herbs or spices, or by adjusting the amount of garlic and Parmesan to suit your taste preferences.

Lemon Herb Baked Cod

Ingredients:

- 4 cod fillets (about 6 ounces each)
- 2 tablespoons olive oil
- Zest and juice of 1 lemon
- 2 cloves garlic, minced
- 1 tablespoon chopped fresh parsley
- 1 tablespoon chopped fresh dill
- Salt and pepper to taste
- Lemon slices for garnish

Instructions:

1. Preheat your oven to 375°F (190°C). Line a baking dish with parchment paper or lightly grease it with olive oil to prevent sticking.
2. In a small bowl, whisk together the olive oil, lemon zest, lemon juice, minced garlic, chopped parsley, chopped dill, salt, and pepper to create a marinade.
3. Place the cod fillets in the prepared baking dish in a single layer.
4. Pour the marinade over the cod fillets, making sure to coat them evenly. You can also use a brush to spread the marinade over the fish.
5. Let the cod marinate in the refrigerator for about 15-30 minutes to allow the flavors to infuse.
6. Once marinated, place the baking dish in the preheated oven and bake the cod for 12-15 minutes, or until the fish is opaque and flakes easily with a fork.
7. If desired, you can broil the cod for an additional 2-3 minutes at the end to lightly brown the top.
8. Remove the baked cod from the oven and let it rest for a few minutes before serving.
9. Garnish the baked cod with lemon slices and additional chopped parsley or dill, if desired.
10. Serve the lemon herb baked cod hot with your favorite side dishes, such as steamed vegetables, rice, or a fresh salad.

Enjoy your delicious and nutritious lemon herb baked cod as a light and satisfying meal!

Quinoa and Vegetable Stuffed Peppers

Ingredients:

- 4 large bell peppers (any color), halved and seeds removed
- 1 cup quinoa, rinsed
- 2 cups vegetable broth or water
- 1 tablespoon olive oil
- 1 onion, diced
- 2 cloves garlic, minced
- 1 carrot, diced
- 1 zucchini, diced
- 1 cup diced tomatoes (fresh or canned)
- 1 cup corn kernels (fresh, frozen, or canned)
- 1 teaspoon ground cumin
- 1 teaspoon paprika
- Salt and pepper to taste
- Optional toppings: shredded cheese, chopped fresh cilantro or parsley, avocado slices, sour cream or Greek yogurt

Instructions:

1. Preheat your oven to 375°F (190°C). Arrange the halved bell peppers in a large baking dish, cut side up.
2. In a medium saucepan, combine the quinoa and vegetable broth or water. Bring to a boil over high heat, then reduce the heat to low, cover, and simmer for 15-20 minutes, or until the quinoa is cooked and the liquid is absorbed. Remove from heat and set aside.
3. While the quinoa is cooking, heat the olive oil in a large skillet over medium heat. Add the diced onion and cook for 3-4 minutes, or until softened.
4. Add the minced garlic, diced carrot, and diced zucchini to the skillet. Cook for another 3-4 minutes, stirring occasionally, until the vegetables are tender.
5. Stir in the diced tomatoes, corn kernels, ground cumin, paprika, salt, and pepper to the skillet. Cook for 2-3 minutes, until the mixture is heated through and well combined.
6. Remove the skillet from the heat and stir in the cooked quinoa until evenly distributed.
7. Spoon the quinoa and vegetable mixture evenly into the halved bell peppers, pressing down gently to pack the filling.

8. Cover the baking dish with aluminum foil and bake in the preheated oven for 25-30 minutes, or until the peppers are tender.
9. Remove the foil from the baking dish and sprinkle the stuffed peppers with shredded cheese, if desired. Return to the oven and bake for an additional 5 minutes, or until the cheese is melted and bubbly.
10. Remove the stuffed peppers from the oven and let them cool for a few minutes before serving.
11. Serve the quinoa and vegetable stuffed peppers hot, garnished with chopped fresh cilantro or parsley, avocado slices, and a dollop of sour cream or Greek yogurt if desired.

Enjoy your delicious quinoa and vegetable stuffed peppers as a satisfying and nutritious meal!

Grilled Vegetable Quinoa Salad

Ingredients:

For the grilled vegetables:

- 2 bell peppers (any color), seeded and quartered
- 1 large zucchini, sliced lengthwise
- 1 large eggplant, sliced into rounds
- 1 red onion, sliced into rounds
- 2 tablespoons olive oil
- Salt and pepper to taste

For the quinoa:

- 1 cup quinoa, rinsed
- 2 cups vegetable broth or water
- Salt to taste

For the dressing:

- 1/4 cup extra virgin olive oil
- 2 tablespoons balsamic vinegar
- 1 tablespoon Dijon mustard
- 1 clove garlic, minced
- 1 teaspoon honey or maple syrup (optional)
- Salt and pepper to taste

Additional ingredients:

- 1/4 cup chopped fresh parsley or basil
- 1/4 cup crumbled feta cheese (optional)
- 1/4 cup toasted pine nuts or chopped almonds (optional)

Instructions:

1. Preheat your grill to medium-high heat.
2. In a large bowl, toss the quartered bell peppers, sliced zucchini, sliced eggplant, and sliced red onion with olive oil, salt, and pepper until evenly coated.

3. Place the vegetables on the preheated grill and cook for 4-5 minutes per side, or until they are tender and have grill marks. Remove from the grill and let them cool slightly.
4. While the vegetables are grilling, prepare the quinoa. In a medium saucepan, combine the rinsed quinoa and vegetable broth or water. Bring to a boil, then reduce the heat to low, cover, and simmer for 15-20 minutes, or until the quinoa is cooked and the liquid is absorbed. Remove from heat and let it sit, covered, for 5 minutes. Fluff with a fork and let it cool slightly.
5. In a small bowl, whisk together the extra virgin olive oil, balsamic vinegar, Dijon mustard, minced garlic, honey or maple syrup (if using), salt, and pepper to make the dressing.
6. In a large mixing bowl, combine the cooked quinoa, grilled vegetables, chopped fresh parsley or basil, and crumbled feta cheese (if using). Drizzle the dressing over the salad and toss gently to combine.
7. If desired, sprinkle toasted pine nuts or chopped almonds over the salad for added crunch.
8. Serve the grilled vegetable quinoa salad at room temperature or chilled.
9. Enjoy your delicious and nutritious grilled vegetable quinoa salad as a light and satisfying meal!

This salad is versatile and can be customized with your favorite vegetables, herbs, and toppings. It's perfect for meal prep and can be enjoyed as a side dish or a main course. Feel free to experiment with different variations to suit your taste preferences.

Herb-Marinated Grilled Chicken Breast

Ingredients:

- 4 boneless, skinless chicken breasts
- 2 tablespoons olive oil
- 2 cloves garlic, minced
- 2 tablespoons chopped fresh herbs (such as rosemary, thyme, parsley, or basil)
- 1 tablespoon lemon juice
- 1 teaspoon lemon zest
- 1 teaspoon Dijon mustard
- Salt and pepper to taste

Instructions:

1. In a small bowl, whisk together the olive oil, minced garlic, chopped fresh herbs, lemon juice, lemon zest, Dijon mustard, salt, and pepper to create the marinade.
2. Place the chicken breasts in a shallow dish or a resealable plastic bag.
3. Pour the marinade over the chicken breasts, making sure they are evenly coated. Massage the marinade into the chicken breasts to ensure they are well seasoned.
4. Cover the dish or seal the bag, and let the chicken marinate in the refrigerator for at least 30 minutes, or up to 4 hours, to allow the flavors to meld together.
5. Preheat your grill to medium-high heat.
6. Remove the chicken breasts from the marinade and discard any excess marinade.
7. Grill the chicken breasts on the preheated grill for 6-8 minutes per side, or until they are cooked through and no longer pink in the center. The internal temperature of the chicken should reach 165°F (75°C).
8. Once the chicken breasts are done grilling, remove them from the grill and let them rest for a few minutes before serving.
9. Serve the herb-marinated grilled chicken breasts hot, garnished with additional chopped fresh herbs if desired.
10. Enjoy your delicious and flavorful herb-marinated grilled chicken breasts as a main course alongside your favorite side dishes!

These chicken breasts are perfect for serving with grilled vegetables, rice, quinoa, or a fresh salad. They're also great for meal prep and can be stored in the refrigerator for a few days, allowing you to enjoy them throughout the week. Feel free to customize the recipe by using your favorite herbs or adding other ingredients to the marinade.

Spicy Black Bean and Vegetable Soup

Ingredients:

- 2 tablespoons olive oil
- 1 onion, diced
- 2 cloves garlic, minced
- 1 bell pepper, diced
- 2 carrots, diced
- 2 stalks celery, diced
- 1 jalapeño pepper, seeded and diced (adjust to taste)
- 2 teaspoons ground cumin
- 1 teaspoon chili powder
- 1/2 teaspoon smoked paprika
- 1/4 teaspoon cayenne pepper (adjust to taste)
- 2 cans (15 ounces each) black beans, drained and rinsed
- 1 can (14.5 ounces) diced tomatoes
- 4 cups vegetable broth
- Salt and pepper to taste
- Juice of 1 lime
- Optional toppings: chopped fresh cilantro, diced avocado, sour cream or Greek yogurt, shredded cheese, lime wedges

Instructions:

1. Heat the olive oil in a large pot or Dutch oven over medium heat.
2. Add the diced onion, minced garlic, diced bell pepper, diced carrots, diced celery, and diced jalapeño pepper to the pot. Cook for 5-7 minutes, stirring occasionally, until the vegetables are softened.
3. Stir in the ground cumin, chili powder, smoked paprika, and cayenne pepper. Cook for another 1-2 minutes, stirring constantly, until the spices are fragrant.
4. Add the drained and rinsed black beans, diced tomatoes (with their juices), and vegetable broth to the pot. Stir to combine.
5. Bring the soup to a simmer, then reduce the heat to low. Cover and let the soup simmer for 20-25 minutes, stirring occasionally, to allow the flavors to meld together.

6. Taste the soup and season with salt and pepper to taste. Adjust the seasoning and spiciness level to your preference by adding more cayenne pepper or jalapeño if desired.
7. Just before serving, stir in the lime juice to brighten up the flavors.
8. Ladle the spicy black bean and vegetable soup into bowls and garnish with your favorite toppings, such as chopped fresh cilantro, diced avocado, sour cream or Greek yogurt, shredded cheese, or lime wedges.
9. Serve the soup hot and enjoy!

This spicy black bean and vegetable soup is perfect for serving as a satisfying and nutritious meal on its own or as a starter for a larger meal. It's also great for meal prep and can be stored in the refrigerator for a few days or frozen for longer storage. Feel free to customize the recipe by adding other vegetables, beans, or spices to suit your taste preferences.

Greek Yogurt Chicken Salad Wraps

Ingredients:

For the chicken salad:

- 2 cups cooked chicken breast, shredded or diced
- 1/2 cup plain Greek yogurt
- 2 tablespoons mayonnaise
- 1 tablespoon Dijon mustard
- 1 stalk celery, finely diced
- 1/4 cup red onion, finely diced
- 1/4 cup chopped fresh parsley
- 1 tablespoon lemon juice
- Salt and pepper to taste

For assembling the wraps:

- Large whole wheat or spinach tortillas
- Leafy greens (such as spinach or lettuce)
- Sliced tomatoes
- Sliced cucumbers
- Optional additions: sliced avocado, shredded carrots, alfalfa sprouts

Instructions:

1. In a large mixing bowl, combine the cooked chicken breast, Greek yogurt, mayonnaise, Dijon mustard, diced celery, diced red onion, chopped fresh parsley, lemon juice, salt, and pepper. Stir until all the ingredients are well combined and the chicken is evenly coated with the dressing.
2. Lay out the tortillas on a clean work surface.
3. Place a few leafy greens in the center of each tortilla, leaving some space around the edges.
4. Spoon the Greek yogurt chicken salad mixture onto the leafy greens, dividing it evenly among the tortillas.
5. Add sliced tomatoes, sliced cucumbers, and any other desired toppings on top of the chicken salad mixture.

6. Fold in the sides of each tortilla, then roll them up tightly from the bottom to create wraps.
7. If desired, slice each wrap in half diagonally before serving.
8. Serve the Greek yogurt chicken salad wraps immediately, or wrap them tightly in foil or parchment paper for a convenient grab-and-go meal.
9. Enjoy your delicious and nutritious Greek yogurt chicken salad wraps as a satisfying and flavorful meal!

These wraps are perfect for a quick and easy lunch or dinner, and they're also great for meal prep. You can customize them by adding your favorite vegetables or herbs, and you can also use whole grain or gluten-free tortillas if desired. Feel free to experiment with different variations to suit your taste preferences!

Lemon Garlic Shrimp and Broccoli Stir-Fry

Ingredients:

- 1 lb large shrimp, peeled and deveined
- 2 tablespoons olive oil
- 4 cloves garlic, minced
- 1 tablespoon grated fresh ginger
- 1 head broccoli, cut into florets
- 1 bell pepper, thinly sliced
- Zest and juice of 1 lemon
- 2 tablespoons soy sauce or tamari
- 1 teaspoon honey or maple syrup
- Salt and pepper to taste
- Optional garnish: chopped green onions, sesame seeds

Instructions:

1. In a small bowl, whisk together the lemon zest, lemon juice, soy sauce or tamari, and honey or maple syrup to create the sauce. Set aside.
2. Heat 1 tablespoon of olive oil in a large skillet or wok over medium-high heat.
3. Add the minced garlic and grated ginger to the skillet, and stir-fry for about 30 seconds, until fragrant.
4. Add the shrimp to the skillet in a single layer, and cook for 2-3 minutes per side, until pink and opaque. Remove the cooked shrimp from the skillet and set aside.
5. In the same skillet, add the remaining tablespoon of olive oil.
6. Add the broccoli florets and sliced bell pepper to the skillet, and stir-fry for 3-4 minutes, until the vegetables are crisp-tender.
7. Return the cooked shrimp to the skillet, and pour the lemon soy sauce mixture over the shrimp and vegetables. Stir to coat everything evenly with the sauce.
8. Cook for an additional 1-2 minutes, until the sauce has thickened slightly and everything is heated through.
9. Season with salt and pepper to taste.
10. Remove the skillet from the heat and garnish with chopped green onions and sesame seeds, if desired.
11. Serve the lemon garlic shrimp and broccoli stir-fry hot over cooked rice or noodles.

12. Enjoy your delicious and flavorful lemon garlic shrimp and broccoli stir-fry as a satisfying and healthy meal!

Feel free to customize this stir-fry with your favorite vegetables or protein options. You can also adjust the seasoning and spice level to suit your taste preferences.

Turkey and Spinach Stuffed Mushrooms

Ingredients:

- 16 large button mushrooms, stems removed and reserved
- 1 tablespoon olive oil
- 1/2 onion, finely chopped
- 2 cloves garlic, minced
- 8 ounces ground turkey
- 2 cups fresh spinach, chopped
- 1/4 cup grated Parmesan cheese
- Salt and pepper to taste
- Optional garnish: chopped fresh parsley or basil

Instructions:

1. Preheat your oven to 375°F (190°C). Line a baking sheet with parchment paper or lightly grease it with olive oil.
2. Clean the mushroom caps with a damp cloth and remove the stems. Finely chop the mushroom stems and set aside.
3. Heat the olive oil in a large skillet over medium heat. Add the chopped onion and minced garlic to the skillet, and cook for 2-3 minutes until softened and fragrant.
4. Add the chopped mushroom stems to the skillet and cook for another 3-4 minutes until they release their moisture and begin to brown.
5. Push the onion, garlic, and mushroom mixture to one side of the skillet and add the ground turkey to the empty side. Cook the turkey, breaking it up with a spoon, until it is browned and cooked through.
6. Stir the cooked turkey into the onion, garlic, and mushroom mixture in the skillet.
7. Add the chopped spinach to the skillet and cook for 2-3 minutes until wilted.
8. Remove the skillet from the heat and stir in the grated Parmesan cheese. Season with salt and pepper to taste.
9. Stuff each mushroom cap with a spoonful of the turkey and spinach mixture, pressing down gently to pack the filling.
10. Place the stuffed mushrooms on the prepared baking sheet in a single layer.
11. Bake in the preheated oven for 15-20 minutes, or until the mushrooms are tender and the filling is heated through.
12. Remove the stuffed mushrooms from the oven and let them cool slightly before serving.

13. Garnish with chopped fresh parsley or basil, if desired.
14. Serve the turkey and spinach stuffed mushrooms warm as a delicious appetizer or snack.

Enjoy your flavorful and satisfying turkey and spinach stuffed mushrooms! They're sure to be a hit at your next gathering.

Mediterranean Tuna Salad Lettuce Wraps

Ingredients:

- 2 cans (5 ounces each) tuna, drained
- 1/4 cup diced red onion
- 1/4 cup diced cucumber
- 1/4 cup diced tomato
- 1/4 cup chopped Kalamata olives
- 2 tablespoons chopped fresh parsley
- 1 tablespoon capers, drained and chopped
- 2 tablespoons extra virgin olive oil
- 1 tablespoon red wine vinegar
- 1 teaspoon Dijon mustard
- Salt and pepper to taste
- Lettuce leaves for wrapping (such as butter lettuce, romaine, or iceberg)

Instructions:

1. In a large mixing bowl, combine the drained tuna, diced red onion, diced cucumber, diced tomato, chopped Kalamata olives, chopped fresh parsley, and chopped capers.
2. In a small bowl, whisk together the extra virgin olive oil, red wine vinegar, Dijon mustard, salt, and pepper to create the dressing.
3. Pour the dressing over the tuna and vegetable mixture in the large mixing bowl. Toss gently to combine, making sure everything is evenly coated with the dressing.
4. Taste the tuna salad and adjust the seasoning with more salt and pepper if needed.
5. Spoon the Mediterranean tuna salad mixture onto individual lettuce leaves, dividing it evenly among them.
6. Wrap the lettuce leaves around the tuna salad filling, folding in the sides to create wraps.
7. Serve the Mediterranean tuna salad lettuce wraps immediately, or refrigerate them for later enjoyment.
8. Enjoy your delicious and nutritious Mediterranean tuna salad lettuce wraps as a light and satisfying meal!

These lettuce wraps are perfect for serving as a quick lunch, a healthy snack, or even as an appetizer for parties or gatherings. They're packed with flavor and nutrients and are sure to be a hit with everyone! Feel free to customize the recipe by adding your favorite ingredients or toppings, such as avocado slices, chopped bell peppers, or feta cheese.

Herb-Roasted Turkey Breast

Ingredients:

- 1 bone-in turkey breast (about 4-6 pounds)
- 2 tablespoons olive oil or melted butter
- 2 cloves garlic, minced
- 1 tablespoon chopped fresh rosemary
- 1 tablespoon chopped fresh thyme
- 1 tablespoon chopped fresh sage
- 1 tablespoon chopped fresh parsley
- 1 teaspoon dried oregano
- 1 teaspoon dried basil
- 1 teaspoon paprika
- Salt and pepper to taste
- 1 lemon, halved
- 1 onion, quartered
- 2 carrots, chopped
- 2 celery stalks, chopped
- 1 cup chicken broth or water

Instructions:

1. Preheat your oven to 350°F (175°C). Place a rack in a roasting pan and lightly grease it with cooking spray or olive oil.
2. In a small bowl, combine the olive oil or melted butter, minced garlic, chopped fresh herbs (rosemary, thyme, sage, parsley), dried oregano, dried basil, paprika, salt, and pepper to create the herb mixture.
3. Rinse the turkey breast under cold water and pat it dry with paper towels. Place the turkey breast on the prepared rack in the roasting pan.
4. Rub the herb mixture all over the turkey breast, making sure to coat it evenly.
5. Squeeze the lemon halves over the turkey breast and place them in the cavity of the bird.
6. Scatter the quartered onion, chopped carrots, and chopped celery around the turkey breast in the roasting pan.
7. Pour the chicken broth or water into the bottom of the roasting pan.
8. Cover the roasting pan with aluminum foil and roast the turkey breast in the preheated oven for about 1 1/2 to 2 hours, or until the internal temperature

reaches 165°F (75°C) when tested with a meat thermometer. Baste the turkey breast with pan juices every 30 minutes or so.
9. Remove the foil during the last 30 minutes of roasting to allow the skin to brown.
10. Once the turkey breast is done roasting, remove it from the oven and let it rest for about 10-15 minutes before slicing.
11. Carve the turkey breast into slices and serve hot with your favorite side dishes.
12. Enjoy your delicious herb-roasted turkey breast as the centerpiece of a festive meal!

This herb-roasted turkey breast is juicy, flavorful, and aromatic, making it a perfect choice for any special occasion. Feel free to customize the herb mixture with your favorite fresh or dried herbs, and adjust the seasoning to suit your taste preferences.

Roasted Cauliflower and Chickpea Salad

Ingredients:

For the salad:

- 1 head cauliflower, cut into florets
- 1 can (15 ounces) chickpeas, drained and rinsed
- 2 tablespoons olive oil
- 1 teaspoon ground cumin
- 1 teaspoon smoked paprika
- 1/2 teaspoon garlic powder
- Salt and pepper to taste
- 4 cups mixed salad greens (such as spinach, arugula, or kale)
- 1/4 cup chopped fresh parsley or cilantro
- 1/4 cup crumbled feta cheese (optional)
- 2 tablespoons toasted pine nuts or chopped almonds (optional)

For the dressing:

- 3 tablespoons extra virgin olive oil
- 2 tablespoons lemon juice
- 1 teaspoon Dijon mustard
- 1 clove garlic, minced
- Salt and pepper to taste

Instructions:

1. Preheat your oven to 425°F (220°C). Line a baking sheet with parchment paper or aluminum foil for easy cleanup.
2. In a large mixing bowl, toss the cauliflower florets and chickpeas with olive oil, ground cumin, smoked paprika, garlic powder, salt, and pepper until evenly coated.
3. Spread the cauliflower and chickpeas out in a single layer on the prepared baking sheet.
4. Roast in the preheated oven for 25-30 minutes, or until the cauliflower is tender and golden brown, and the chickpeas are crispy, stirring halfway through cooking.

5. While the cauliflower and chickpeas are roasting, prepare the dressing. In a small bowl, whisk together the extra virgin olive oil, lemon juice, Dijon mustard, minced garlic, salt, and pepper until emulsified. Set aside.
6. Once the cauliflower and chickpeas are done roasting, remove them from the oven and let them cool slightly.
7. In a large salad bowl, combine the roasted cauliflower and chickpeas with the mixed salad greens and chopped fresh parsley or cilantro.
8. Drizzle the dressing over the salad and toss gently to coat everything evenly.
9. If using, sprinkle crumbled feta cheese and toasted pine nuts or chopped almonds over the salad.
10. Serve the roasted cauliflower and chickpea salad immediately as a side or a light main course.
11. Enjoy your flavorful and nutritious roasted cauliflower and chickpea salad!

This salad is versatile and can be customized with your favorite ingredients and toppings. Feel free to add other vegetables, herbs, or protein options to suit your taste preferences. It's perfect for meal prep and can be enjoyed as a healthy lunch or dinner option throughout the week.

Grilled Lemon Herb Salmon

Ingredients:

- 4 salmon fillets (about 6 ounces each), skin-on or skinless
- 2 tablespoons olive oil
- Zest and juice of 1 lemon
- 2 cloves garlic, minced
- 2 tablespoons chopped fresh herbs (such as dill, parsley, or thyme)
- Salt and pepper to taste
- Lemon slices for garnish

Instructions:

1. Preheat your grill to medium-high heat. If using a charcoal grill, make sure the coals are hot and have turned gray.
2. In a small bowl, whisk together the olive oil, lemon zest, lemon juice, minced garlic, chopped fresh herbs, salt, and pepper to create the marinade.
3. Place the salmon fillets in a shallow dish or a resealable plastic bag.
4. Pour the marinade over the salmon fillets, making sure they are evenly coated. Massage the marinade into the salmon fillets to ensure they are well seasoned.
5. Cover the dish or seal the bag, and let the salmon marinate in the refrigerator for at least 30 minutes, or up to 1 hour, to allow the flavors to meld together.
6. Remove the salmon fillets from the marinade and discard any excess marinade.
7. Place the salmon fillets directly on the grill grates, skin-side down if using skin-on fillets.
8. Grill the salmon for 4-5 minutes per side, depending on the thickness of the fillets, or until they are cooked to your desired level of doneness. The internal temperature of the salmon should reach 145°F (63°C) when tested with a meat thermometer.
9. Once the salmon is done grilling, remove it from the grill and let it rest for a few minutes before serving.
10. Garnish the grilled lemon herb salmon with lemon slices and additional chopped fresh herbs if desired.
11. Serve the grilled lemon herb salmon hot with your favorite side dishes, such as grilled vegetables, rice, or a fresh salad.
12. Enjoy your delicious and flavorful grilled lemon herb salmon as a light and satisfying meal!

This grilled salmon is perfect for summer cookouts, but you can also cook it indoors on a grill pan or in the oven if needed. Feel free to customize the recipe by using your favorite herbs or adding other ingredients to the marinade.

Lentil and Vegetable Stuffed Bell Peppers

Ingredients:

- 4 large bell peppers (any color), halved and seeds removed
- 1 cup dry green or brown lentils, rinsed
- 2 cups vegetable broth or water
- 2 tablespoons olive oil
- 1 onion, diced
- 2 cloves garlic, minced
- 2 carrots, diced
- 2 stalks celery, diced
- 1 zucchini, diced
- 1 cup diced tomatoes (fresh or canned)
- 1 cup cooked quinoa or rice
- 2 teaspoons dried Italian seasoning
- Salt and pepper to taste
- Optional toppings: shredded cheese, chopped fresh parsley or basil

Instructions:

1. Preheat your oven to 375°F (190°C). Arrange the halved bell peppers in a baking dish, cut side up.
2. In a medium saucepan, combine the rinsed lentils and vegetable broth or water. Bring to a boil over high heat, then reduce the heat to low, cover, and simmer for 20-25 minutes, or until the lentils are tender and the liquid is absorbed. Remove from heat and set aside.
3. While the lentils are cooking, heat the olive oil in a large skillet over medium heat. Add the diced onion and cook for 3-4 minutes, or until softened.
4. Add the minced garlic, diced carrots, diced celery, and diced zucchini to the skillet. Cook for another 5-6 minutes, stirring occasionally, until the vegetables are tender.
5. Stir in the diced tomatoes, cooked lentils, cooked quinoa or rice, dried Italian seasoning, salt, and pepper to the skillet. Cook for 2-3 minutes, until everything is heated through and well combined. Adjust seasoning to taste.
6. Spoon the lentil and vegetable mixture evenly into the halved bell peppers, pressing down gently to pack the filling.
7. Cover the baking dish with aluminum foil and bake in the preheated oven for 25-30 minutes, or until the peppers are tender.

8. If desired, remove the foil during the last 10 minutes of baking to allow the tops to brown slightly.
9. Remove the stuffed peppers from the oven and let them cool for a few minutes before serving.
10. Garnish the lentil and vegetable stuffed bell peppers with shredded cheese and chopped fresh parsley or basil, if desired.
11. Serve the stuffed peppers hot as a delicious and satisfying meal!

These lentil and vegetable stuffed bell peppers are packed with flavor and nutrients, making them a great choice for a vegetarian dinner option. Feel free to customize the recipe by using your favorite vegetables or adding other ingredients to the filling. Enjoy!

Baked Chicken with Tomato and Basil

Ingredients:

- 4 boneless, skinless chicken breasts
- Salt and pepper to taste
- 2 tablespoons olive oil
- 2 cloves garlic, minced
- 1 can (14.5 ounces) diced tomatoes, drained
- 1/4 cup chopped fresh basil leaves
- 1/4 cup grated Parmesan cheese
- Optional: additional fresh basil leaves for garnish

Instructions:

1. Preheat your oven to 375°F (190°C).
2. Season the chicken breasts with salt and pepper on both sides.
3. In a large oven-proof skillet or baking dish, heat the olive oil over medium-high heat.
4. Add the seasoned chicken breasts to the skillet and cook for 2-3 minutes on each side, or until lightly browned. Remove the chicken breasts from the skillet and set aside.
5. In the same skillet, add the minced garlic and cook for 1 minute, until fragrant.
6. Add the diced tomatoes to the skillet and cook for another 2-3 minutes, stirring occasionally.
7. Return the chicken breasts to the skillet, nestling them into the tomato mixture.
8. Sprinkle the chopped fresh basil leaves over the chicken breasts.
9. Transfer the skillet to the preheated oven and bake for 20-25 minutes, or until the chicken is cooked through and no longer pink in the center. The internal temperature of the chicken should reach 165°F (75°C) when tested with a meat thermometer.
10. Sprinkle the grated Parmesan cheese over the chicken breasts during the last 5 minutes of baking, allowing it to melt and become golden brown.
11. Once the chicken is done baking, remove the skillet from the oven and let it rest for a few minutes before serving.
12. Garnish the baked chicken with additional fresh basil leaves, if desired.
13. Serve the baked chicken with tomato and basil hot, accompanied by your favorite side dishes, such as pasta, rice, or a salad.

Enjoy your delicious and flavorful baked chicken with tomato and basil! It's a simple and satisfying dish that's perfect for a weeknight dinner or a special occasion.

Quinoa and Kale Salad with Lemon Vinaigrette

Ingredients:

For the salad:

- 1 cup quinoa, rinsed
- 2 cups water or vegetable broth
- 1 bunch kale, stems removed and leaves thinly sliced
- 1/2 cup sliced almonds, toasted
- 1/4 cup dried cranberries or raisins
- 1/4 cup crumbled feta cheese (optional)
- Salt and pepper to taste

For the lemon vinaigrette:

- 1/4 cup extra virgin olive oil
- 2 tablespoons fresh lemon juice
- 1 teaspoon lemon zest
- 1 clove garlic, minced
- 1 teaspoon Dijon mustard
- 1 teaspoon honey or maple syrup
- Salt and pepper to taste

Instructions:

1. In a medium saucepan, combine the rinsed quinoa and water or vegetable broth. Bring to a boil over high heat, then reduce the heat to low, cover, and simmer for 15-20 minutes, or until the quinoa is cooked and the liquid is absorbed. Remove from heat and let it cool slightly.
2. While the quinoa is cooking, prepare the kale by removing the tough stems and thinly slicing the leaves. Place the sliced kale in a large mixing bowl.
3. In a small skillet, toast the sliced almonds over medium heat until lightly golden and fragrant, stirring frequently to prevent burning. Remove from heat and let them cool.
4. Once the quinoa is cooked, fluff it with a fork and add it to the bowl with the sliced kale.

5. Add the toasted sliced almonds and dried cranberries or raisins to the bowl with the quinoa and kale.
6. If using, add the crumbled feta cheese to the bowl.
7. In a small bowl, whisk together the extra virgin olive oil, fresh lemon juice, lemon zest, minced garlic, Dijon mustard, honey or maple syrup, salt, and pepper to create the lemon vinaigrette.
8. Pour the lemon vinaigrette over the quinoa, kale, and other ingredients in the mixing bowl. Toss gently to coat everything evenly with the dressing.
9. Taste the salad and adjust the seasoning with more salt and pepper if needed.
10. Serve the quinoa and kale salad with lemon vinaigrette immediately as a light and refreshing meal or side dish.
11. Enjoy your delicious and nutritious quinoa and kale salad with lemon vinaigrette!

This salad is perfect for meal prep and can be stored in the refrigerator for a few days, allowing the flavors to meld together even more. Feel free to customize the recipe by adding other ingredients such as diced bell peppers, shredded carrots, or sliced avocado.

Grilled Vegetable Quinoa Bowls

Ingredients:

For the grilled vegetables:

- 2 bell peppers, sliced into strips
- 1 zucchini, sliced
- 1 yellow squash, sliced
- 1 red onion, sliced
- 8 ounces mushrooms, sliced
- 2 tablespoons olive oil
- Salt and pepper to taste
- Optional: other vegetables such as eggplant, asparagus, or cherry tomatoes

For the quinoa:

- 1 cup quinoa, rinsed
- 2 cups water or vegetable broth
- Salt to taste

For the dressing:

- 1/4 cup extra virgin olive oil
- 2 tablespoons balsamic vinegar
- 1 tablespoon honey or maple syrup
- 1 clove garlic, minced
- 1 teaspoon Dijon mustard
- Salt and pepper to taste

Optional toppings:

- Crumbled feta cheese
- Fresh herbs (such as parsley or basil)
- Toasted pine nuts or chopped almonds
- Avocado slices

Instructions:

1. Preheat your grill to medium-high heat. If using a charcoal grill, make sure the coals are hot and have turned gray.
2. In a large bowl, toss the sliced vegetables with olive oil, salt, and pepper until evenly coated.
3. Place the vegetables on the preheated grill in a single layer, making sure they are not too crowded. Grill for 5-7 minutes per side, or until they are tender and have grill marks. Remove from the grill and set aside.
4. While the vegetables are grilling, prepare the quinoa. In a medium saucepan, combine the rinsed quinoa and water or vegetable broth. Bring to a boil over high heat, then reduce the heat to low, cover, and simmer for 15-20 minutes, or until the quinoa is cooked and the liquid is absorbed. Remove from heat and let it cool slightly.
5. In a small bowl, whisk together the ingredients for the dressing: extra virgin olive oil, balsamic vinegar, honey or maple syrup, minced garlic, Dijon mustard, salt, and pepper.
6. Once the quinoa is cooked, fluff it with a fork and divide it among serving bowls.
7. Arrange the grilled vegetables on top of the quinoa in each bowl.
8. Drizzle the dressing over the grilled vegetable quinoa bowls.
9. If desired, top the bowls with crumbled feta cheese, fresh herbs, toasted pine nuts or chopped almonds, and avocado slices.
10. Serve the grilled vegetable quinoa bowls immediately and enjoy!

These bowls are versatile and customizable, so feel free to mix and match your favorite grilled vegetables and toppings. They're perfect for a healthy and satisfying lunch or dinner option that's sure to please everyone!

Turkey and Vegetable Skillet

Ingredients:

- 1 lb ground turkey
- 2 tablespoons olive oil
- 1 onion, diced
- 2 cloves garlic, minced
- 2 carrots, diced
- 2 celery stalks, diced
- 1 bell pepper, diced
- 1 zucchini, diced
- 1 teaspoon dried oregano
- 1 teaspoon dried basil
- 1 teaspoon paprika
- Salt and pepper to taste
- 1 can (14.5 ounces) diced tomatoes, undrained
- Optional: grated cheese, chopped fresh herbs for garnish

Instructions:

1. Heat olive oil in a large skillet over medium heat. Add diced onion and minced garlic, and sauté for 2-3 minutes until fragrant.
2. Add ground turkey to the skillet and cook, breaking it up with a spoon, until browned and cooked through.
3. Add diced carrots, celery, bell pepper, and zucchini to the skillet. Cook for 5-7 minutes, stirring occasionally, until the vegetables are tender.
4. Season the mixture with dried oregano, dried basil, paprika, salt, and pepper. Stir well to combine.
5. Pour the diced tomatoes with their juices into the skillet. Stir to combine with the turkey and vegetable mixture.
6. Simmer the skillet for 5-10 minutes, allowing the flavors to meld together and the sauce to thicken slightly.
7. Taste and adjust seasoning as needed.
8. If desired, sprinkle grated cheese over the top of the skillet and cover with a lid for a few minutes until the cheese is melted.
9. Serve the turkey and vegetable skillet hot, garnished with chopped fresh herbs if desired.

10. Enjoy your delicious and nutritious turkey and vegetable skillet!

This dish is versatile, and you can customize it with your favorite vegetables and seasonings. It's perfect for a quick weeknight dinner and leftovers can be enjoyed for lunch the next day.

Lemon Herb Baked Chicken Thighs

Ingredients:

- 6 bone-in, skin-on chicken thighs
- 2 tablespoons olive oil
- Zest and juice of 1 lemon
- 2 cloves garlic, minced
- 1 tablespoon chopped fresh herbs (such as thyme, rosemary, or parsley)
- Salt and pepper to taste
- Lemon slices for garnish

Instructions:

1. Preheat your oven to 400°F (200°C). Line a baking sheet with parchment paper or aluminum foil for easy cleanup.
2. In a small bowl, whisk together the olive oil, lemon zest, lemon juice, minced garlic, chopped fresh herbs, salt, and pepper to create the marinade.
3. Pat the chicken thighs dry with paper towels and place them in a large mixing bowl.
4. Pour the marinade over the chicken thighs, making sure they are evenly coated. Massage the marinade into the chicken thighs to ensure they are well seasoned.
5. Arrange the chicken thighs on the prepared baking sheet, skin-side up.
6. Place a lemon slice on top of each chicken thigh for added flavor and garnish.
7. Bake the chicken thighs in the preheated oven for 30-35 minutes, or until they are golden brown and the internal temperature reaches 165°F (75°C) when tested with a meat thermometer.
8. Once the chicken thighs are done baking, remove them from the oven and let them rest for a few minutes before serving.
9. Serve the lemon herb baked chicken thighs hot, accompanied by your favorite side dishes, such as roasted vegetables, mashed potatoes, or a fresh salad.
10. Enjoy your delicious and flavorful lemon herb baked chicken thighs!

This dish is versatile, and you can customize it with your favorite herbs and seasonings. It's perfect for a family dinner or entertaining guests, and leftovers can be enjoyed the next day as well.

Mediterranean Eggplant and Tomato Bake

Ingredients:

- 2 medium eggplants, sliced into 1/4-inch rounds
- 3 large tomatoes, sliced into 1/4-inch rounds
- 1 onion, thinly sliced
- 3 cloves garlic, minced
- 1/4 cup chopped fresh basil leaves
- 1/4 cup chopped fresh parsley leaves
- 1/4 cup chopped fresh oregano leaves
- 1/4 cup extra virgin olive oil
- Salt and pepper to taste
- 1/2 cup crumbled feta cheese (optional)
- Optional garnish: fresh basil leaves, chopped parsley

Instructions:

1. Preheat your oven to 375°F (190°C). Lightly grease a baking dish with olive oil or cooking spray.
2. Arrange the sliced eggplants in a single layer on the bottom of the baking dish.
3. Sprinkle the minced garlic and thinly sliced onion over the eggplant slices.
4. Drizzle half of the extra virgin olive oil over the eggplant, garlic, and onion. Sprinkle half of the chopped fresh basil, parsley, and oregano over the top. Season with salt and pepper to taste.
5. Layer the sliced tomatoes over the eggplant mixture.
6. Drizzle the remaining olive oil over the tomatoes. Sprinkle the remaining chopped herbs over the top. Season with salt and pepper again.
7. Cover the baking dish with aluminum foil and bake in the preheated oven for 25-30 minutes, or until the vegetables are tender and cooked through.
8. If using, sprinkle the crumbled feta cheese over the top of the baked vegetables during the last 5 minutes of baking, allowing it to melt slightly.
9. Once the vegetables are done baking, remove the baking dish from the oven and let it cool slightly.
10. Garnish the Mediterranean eggplant and tomato bake with fresh basil leaves and chopped parsley, if desired.
11. Serve the dish hot as a delicious and flavorful main course or side dish.
12. Enjoy your Mediterranean eggplant and tomato bake!

This dish is perfect for showcasing the vibrant flavors of the Mediterranean. It's great served alongside grilled meats, fish, or as a vegetarian main dish. Feel free to customize the recipe by adding your favorite herbs or vegetables.

Herb-Marinated Grilled Pork Tenderloin

Ingredients:

- 2 pork tenderloins (about 1 to 1.5 pounds each)
- 1/4 cup olive oil
- 2 tablespoons balsamic vinegar
- 2 cloves garlic, minced
- 2 teaspoons chopped fresh rosemary
- 2 teaspoons chopped fresh thyme
- 2 teaspoons chopped fresh parsley
- 1 teaspoon chopped fresh sage
- Salt and pepper to taste

Instructions:

1. In a small bowl, whisk together the olive oil, balsamic vinegar, minced garlic, chopped fresh herbs (rosemary, thyme, parsley, sage), salt, and pepper to create the marinade.
2. Place the pork tenderloins in a large resealable plastic bag or a shallow dish.
3. Pour the marinade over the pork tenderloins, making sure they are evenly coated. Seal the bag or cover the dish, and refrigerate for at least 1 hour, or up to 24 hours, to allow the flavors to meld together.
4. Preheat your grill to medium-high heat. If using a charcoal grill, make sure the coals are hot and have turned gray.
5. Remove the pork tenderloins from the marinade and discard any excess marinade.
6. Grill the pork tenderloins on the preheated grill, turning occasionally, until they are browned on all sides and cooked through. The internal temperature of the pork should reach 145°F (63°C) when tested with a meat thermometer, and there should be a slight blush of pink in the center.
7. Once the pork tenderloins are done grilling, remove them from the grill and let them rest for a few minutes before slicing.
8. Slice the grilled pork tenderloins into thick slices and serve hot.
9. Enjoy your delicious and flavorful herb-marinated grilled pork tenderloin!

This dish pairs well with a variety of side dishes, such as roasted vegetables, mashed potatoes, or a fresh salad. It's perfect for entertaining guests or for a special family dinner. Feel free to customize the recipe by using your favorite herbs or adding other seasonings to the marinade.